# COURAGE
## NOT just a word

PRIYANKA GUPTA

First Published in March 2022

**ISBN: 978-93-93809-89-6**

**BLUEROSE PUBLISHERS**

www.bluerosepublishers.com

info@bluerosepublishers.com

+91 8882 898 898

**Cover Design:**

Akash Bartwal

**Typographic Design:**

Pooja Sharma

**Distributed by:** BlueRose, Amazon, Flipkart

*Beloved mother, who is still my angel, my best friend*

# Contents

# GLIOBLASTOMA– The Villain

**Life is not what we decide; it is what He decides for us.**

Yes, it is a surprising thing, but it is true. In life, we humans love someone so much that we are not able to see the truth and want to believe in the illusion. Even I wanted to believe in illusions because the truth was very painful.

The afternoon of June 9, 2021, was when my entire life was turned into a nightmare. The news broke me from the inside so badly that I lost my senses; I was totally blank, I had no idea how to react. I hugged my mom tightly and said, "Please don't go, as I cannot imagine my life without you." I still remember that night, I was crying and praying to the almighty to give her good health as she is a good human being and her family loves her a lot; she has seen lots of struggles in her life. "If you want to take someone, then take me, not her," I said to God. Unknown to the fact, my mom was smiling and turning her hands over me. That day, she was detected with 'GLIOBLASTOMA', a cancerous brain tumor for which there is no cure till now. Doctors suggested surgery, as with this, they can buy one month extra. But surgery was a highly risky affair, anything could happen, but thankfully, the surgery was successful on 29th June. On that day our happiness seemed to know no limit, but nobody could predict the future. Soon after one week, an infection caught her, and she was rushed to the hospital, with no idea that a real 'HELL' was waiting for us. She was bedridden, not able to speak much; there was no place in her body where needles weren't poked. Her entire body was swollen and turned bluish. But whenever she was in a sense, she used to talk about me.

It is always said that 'Life always gives an out of syllabus question, which you have to pass in any condition.' My struggle started with my inner sense and reality; every day my family used to say that there is very limited time left with mom and anytime anything can happen, and my belief was that nothing will happen to her. As she was a true fighter, a very courageous woman who wanted to see her daughter settle down and be happy. For this, she was fighting daily with God and used to buy some time. I remember when she was in the hospital, she used to say that her daughter is her pride. Everyone including the doctors knew me. I was helpless and cursed myself that I was not able to fulfil her dream.

Nowadays, tarot card reading, astrology, these things are in fashion, thanks to our media houses. When I didn't find any solution from medical science, I became more superstitious and was drawn towards all these things, including black magic, with a belief that at least this thing can do something for her. But trust me, all of these are fake.

A chameleon changes its colour when it finds itself in danger, and we humans change our colours when we find someone in trouble and pain. The finger-pointing started when everyone came to know about my mom's health. It felt that everyone in this universe had got a power of attorney to say anything to me. Whoever used to call or visit to ask about her health used to blame me for her condition; as I was unmarried, and my marriage was constantly in my mother's mind. It was very heart-breaking when her best friend blamed me when my mom was in a very critical condition and had been admitted in the ICU. I slowly started believing that I am responsible and started hating myself. Not only that, but I also tried to commit suicide, but unfortunately, I failed. Trust me, the diluted floor cleaner is of no use.

A call from my friend that changed my thinking; a friend who normally is not in touch with me but has been there during my bad times. A call by that friend always does some magic and helps me gain confidence. A BIG THANK YOU, but it's another thing that after that I didn't receive any call. Well, going forward, after almost two months in the hospital, my mom came home, but in an ambulance, since by that time she was totally bedridden. But I was very happy, as I had seen a smile on her face after such a long time. For a few days, everything was alright; she was recovering and my belief in God was getting firm. But after a few days, her health was again going down, but this time we were not able to take her to the hospital where her treatment was going on, as they have already replied. One day, her health deteriorated, and we rushed her to a nearby hospital, as due to the pandemic, no doctors were ready to pay a home visit; it felt like there was no empathy left. After going to the hospital, doctors informed us about her critical condition. I remember how I was running here and there to talk to doctors, pleading to them to do something. Soon after an argument related to their protocol, she was shifted to the ICU, where after some time, she said her final goodbye. I was shocked and was kissing her on her forehead, pressing her heart, requesting her to please get up, rubbing her feet and hand, hugging her like a small baby, waiting for a MIRACLE to happen but nothing happened. I was repeatedly begging the doctors and the nurses to do something as I was getting the feeling that she was still breathing. But it was too late, and nobody was listening. 28th September, 3:55 pm, was the black day of my life. It broke me and changed me as a person;

suddenly the child in me was dead and a very mature person was born whom I had never met before.

Life after Mom was very difficult as I had lost my motive to live. I did not know what to do. People who used to visit our home were still very insensitive and blamed me, as my mom's last wish was to see me settled and it remained unfulfilled. They blamed me without knowing the fact that I tried my level best but failed miserably. Just to make sure that her last dream comes true, I also tried to do contract marriage, but unfortunately, I failed in that as well. I was listening to all these things in front of my family members. I lost trust in God and was cursing myself for having believed in something that never existed. Deep inside somewhere, I was waiting for a call from that friend, who sometimes called me, but that call didn't come unless I texted after more than a month. Finally, that call came, and I burst into tears like anything; I remember I was sobbing inconsolably. After talking to my angel friend for some time, my life was back on track.

This reminded me about her second biggest happiness. It was just a few years before my parents' 60$^{th}$ anniversary and she was super excited about that. She was planning for the celebration from then onwards, she used to joke by saying, "By that time, my daughter will settle down and will come with her husband to my anniversary party." But it is said that planned things never happen. I remember how my father missed her terribly on 4$^{th}$ December, as it was their 46$^{th}$ marriage anniversary; a pain which can't be explained in words and a loss which cannot be filled by anything.

The word ORPHAN seems to be only a six-letter word but ask a person who lives with this feeling. It breaks you from the inside so badly that you start doubting your own capabilities. Someone has wisely said, "Your life's result will depend on what you feel from inside." While writing this black chapter of my life, I am taken back to the good memories which I had spent with my mom and some horrible incidents that had taken place during this time .

MOM, I know you are watching me, just want to let you know that I have always worshipped you and have loved you unconditionally. Miss you every second, thank you for being my mom and giving me good values in my life and if possible, please COME BACK.

# Our Indian Doctors

**"Every Profession is a noble profession, but it depends on the person and how much they are loyal towards their work"**

It was 1[st] February 2021, when Mom was admitted to the hospital, as she was a COPD patient; her oxygen levels used to be low, but that day, her levels drastically plummeted, and she had to be admitted to the hospital. Before you think what COPD is, let me tell you, it's a disease where a person's lungs don't work as expected and they sometimes need artificial oxygen as support; also, it progresses with age. Many people confuse it with asthma, despite the fact that the two disorders are not the same. Being admitted to the hospital for almost 22 days and repeatedly complaining about headache while freezing suddenly, doctors took it very lightly and didn't gave a thought for an MRI or a brain scan. Let me tell you that these doctors were not ordinary doctors, they were specialized pulmonologists who deal with COPD patients. and out of them some still come on news channels to speak about COPD and its consequences. They also have their own YouTube channels, virtual programmes, etc. If they could have given a thought, at least something could have happened.

Even after getting discharged from the hospital, these things continued. There was an incident where she was having her dinner and suddenly, she froze, and we all panicked, but after a few minutes, she was normal and asked what had happened? "Why are you panicking?"

At this moment, we decided not to depend on the present doctor and consult another doctor.

In March, the appointment of one of the renowned doctors, who had an experience of more than two decades, was made. After consulting her, for a few days, her health was fine, and we took a sigh of relief seeing her smiling. But after a few days again, the freezing thing started and there was a change in her attitude and speech. Despite conveying these symptoms, the doctor still instructed us to give 20-23 hours of oxygen daily. She also said that her speech had changed as a result of her age. Let me remind you that she was just 63 years old, while the doctor was 60. "No one is immortal," she had also declared.

After a few sessions with her, and seeing no improvement in mom's health, we decided to consult a neurologist on June 7th. We got an appointment at Fortis Hospital. On June 8th, as soon as the doctor examined her, he immediately requested a brain scan.

I clearly remember, it was raining heavily and we could barely see the roads, and the cherry on the cake were the potholes. In India, if we want to enjoy the camel ride, we don't have to visit Rajasthan especially, or any other desert of the world, thanks to the potholes, which are, unfortunately, easily available anywhere in our country. We can enjoy a much better ride and that too for free.

Well, coming back to the story; soon, she was taken inside the scanning room and we were waiting in the reception area. Suddenly the receptionist told us that the doctor has seen some doubts of the tumor and another scan named, 'Tumor Scan' needs to be done. Listening to this, we got afraid and soon called the doctor. He said, "It is just a doubt, and to root it out, we need to perform this test."

That entire night, I didn't sleep and prayed to God to please help us and bless her. But I think my prayer was not heard, and the doctor's doubt came true. A devil came into our life to destroy everything.

The report arrived the following day, on the 9th of June, at about 1 p.m. I was out at the time; I was utterly numb as soon as I got the report and sat on the road for an unknown amount of time.

After going through this incident, I remember a funny story, which I am sure every one of us has heard in our childhood.

There was a very famous geography professor who was standing on the road and someone like us asked him what 2+2 is. He looked towards the man and said, 'I am not a maths professor; if you want to know anything about directions, ask me; I will tell you in detail.' A small boy of age 5 was listening to this conversation, and very sweetly he said, 'Uncle 2+2 is 4, and 2*2 is also 4.'

This is how our doctors are. They are specialized in their field so much that they don't want to see the other causes. When they see a symptom, they are not ready to believe that it can be because of other diseases as well.

Have you seen any cab driver who doesn't know the route, but still says yes? They do so because they want to earn money. Sad but true, our dear doctors are also the same; even though they know that this cannot be treated by them, they still treat that person, because they want to earn. Not all doctors are the same, but many are. If any doctor is reading this, I want to urge one thing: please don't do this, because you will only earn money, but someone will lose their loved one, who is their entire universe.

But you also can't blame the doctors. The medical education fees are so much that even they have to waive off their educational loan, and we are just a source of income for them. In this world, all that matters is money, not emotions.

If this was detected early, my mom could have been saved and her family who was crying and missing her terribly could have smiled.

After this incident, I have learned one thing; never trust the doctors blindly, don't go by their ratings, because it is purchased, and never go by their experience, because as days go by, the count of experience increases .

**Take care of your loved ones and stay away from toxicity.**

# A Journey towards Being an Orthodox

**It is wisely said that for getting out of any worse situation, we humans can do anything.**

As soon as my friends came to know about my mother's health condition, one of my friends called and gave me a reference of a woman who performs rituals, and any person whose life is in danger can be saved. With lots of hope I called, and she assured me that nothing will happen to my mom and she will be saved. She also narrated her story about how she saved her parents during the pandemic when doctors had said that they were not going to survive.

I was overjoyed as I listened to this, and I answered yes. She demanded a large sum of money, which I promised to pay and even handed over. She also requested a recent photo of my mum, which I gave her. .

After a few days, she called me and said that someone has done black magic on her and that is the reason she got this tumor. Listening to this, I was very afraid as I was totally new to this MARKET. Yes, you heard this right, I said MARKET; you will come to know the reason very soon.

Someone told me about a renowned pandit who could make anything happen. After calling him, he explained that her planets are out of alignment, which is why this is happening. He just needs to execute a few rites, and she'll be OK. However, this was a challenging task. I wasn't really allowed to eat or drink anything while this procedure was in progress. Nevertheless, I consented. This went on for approximately three days, during that time I didn't have anything and prayed for MOM every second.

Then I was told that if I prayed while standing on one foot, God would grant her life and everything would be well, and a MIRACLE would occur.

Then someone told me that every Tuesday, I had to chant from 1 a.m. to 6 a.m. and fast for one day.

And believe me, for these suggestions, those NOBLE people were charging me a lot.

My condition was so bad that I was ready to eat pebbles from the road and was ready to give my own life too.

Every new person to whom I would contact was giving some new suggestion and like a helpless person, I did everything.

I used to cry the entire night and would get afraid when any call from the hospital used to come.

" You give me one lakh rupees, and I will do liturgy for your mother, and your mother will be safe," someone remarked one day. However, once she is well, you must go barefoot and visit a temple.' That temple was approximately 150 kilometres from my house. But once I hung up the phone, I realised that no faith teaches this. Then I read a lot of religious texts and couldn't find anything like this. My eyes were awakened that day, and I stopped seeking advice from such wise people.

These AGENTS OF GOD used to charge like crazy for suggesting anything to me. Every third person in the world wants to make quick money, and this profession was ideal for that.

People visit this place out of fear and buy invisible merchandise that they can't see most of the time.

If you remember, I had called all this stuff MARKET, because in this MARKET, literally, bargaining is going on. For tarot card reading, 15 mins, 1000 to 1500 Rs, which is negotiable if you show the poor factor. For reiki, it is from 3000 to 1 lakh, depending on how old that person is in this MARKET and what rating they have. For astrology, it is from 500 Rs to 10,000 Rs which again, depends on their market value and so on. Nowadays, they have a call center too, where you can call them and ask any question. I am sure you must have seen such advertisements on many social media platforms.

But, believe me those days where we can find genuine people with expertise who can actually help others are long gone. Today, it's just a business for them, with a lot of competition. My only advice is to avoid becoming entangled in the labyrinth of these good people. They are harmful to our health, our finances, and even for our lives.

# Shocked

**Hammering can break big stones into pieces, which cannot be turned back into their original shape.**

Prior to this incident, I was content with my own tiny world with my mom and nephews, who meant the world to me. Other family members were important, they were particularly so. I remember how much I used to play and cause mischief.

Being the youngest in the family, I was pampered and was mom's favourite child.

I used to think about what I could do for Mom at all hours of the day and night, and how I could make her happy and proud. What could I do to ensure that her lungs begin to function properly?

If a new restaurant opened in my town, I'd be the first to go with her. We pretended to be mother and daughter when, in fact, we were closest friends. I don't think anyone can crack the jokes that I used to crack with her.

My mother, I recall, wanted to throw a big party for my birthday. "My poor daughter never celebrated her birthday," she used to lament. She phoned the entire building, as well as a large number of other guests because she was so delighted that day. She even asked everyone who attended the celebration to pray for me. I believe she knew it was my last birthday with her. But Mom, I will never celebrate my birthday without you; there will be no occasion without you. I miss you, and I know how precious I am to you; if at all possible, please come see me on my birthdays, or take me to your new planet so that I can stay with you. Please take me with you.

I used to be really overweight until June 9th, but as soon as this news arrived and I was informed of the true situation, I didn't respond, and my weight began to drop. I recall not having anything for nearly a week because I forgot. I was thinking this was a nightmare and that I'll be waking up shortly. Still, I believe I'm having a nasty dream that I'd like to wake up from as soon as possible.

I recall her being admitted to the hospital prior to her surgery. She attempted to speak, but due to word mismatches, no one could understand her. My father and sister-in-law used to stay in the hospital, and I was given the responsibility of staying and caring for my nephews because they were kids who needed someone to look after them.

Before the surgery, she threw tantrums where she removed the food pipe from her nose and forcefully came home, that too, without being formally discharged from the hospital. After coming home, she was very happy, and I was just looking at her. I kept my head on  her lap and started crying and I don't know when I slept or fainted.

My attitude towards things changed; I started perceiving things negatively.  For countless nights, I used to stay awake, used to talk to myself to find the answer to why? Why did this happen? Whose mistake is this? Am I responsible? Am I a good daughter? Do I really deserve her love? And many other things.

I still remember she called her brother and said that now it is his responsibility that her daughter gets settled. She started saying how much she is proud of me. And I was looking at her blankly and thinking, do I deserve this love? Because if I was a good daughter this thing would never have happened.

I have this storm inside me. Even during her surgery on 29th June, I didn't go to the hospital. I was there to take care of my nephews, as mom told me that you need to take care, but it was just an excuse; the real reason was, I was unable to see my mom in pain. I lost my senses and didn't know how to react. I wanted to yell and cry my heart out but was not able to.

I used to fold my hands and cry in front of God and say, " Please get her well soon, give her life. She is a very good human, who has always helped others before her and has always thought of others' feelings. If you want to take someone, take me , not her." To be honest, I used to beg.

The surgery was successful and almost 85% of the tumor was removed and the remaining 15%, they were planning to remove it through radiation. We were very happy and jumping out of joy that now nothing will happen to her and had started making plans that once she has fully recovered, we will go for long holidays and throw a party, and many other good things. After one week, she was discharged from the hospital and came home on the 5th of July. I still remember I had made *upma* for her, as that was one of her favourite foods. She looked at me and started feeding me with her own hand. I used to normally sit down beside her. That day also, I sat beside her and she was patting my head after so many days. I was so relieved and happy as my mom was sitting next to me.

I enjoy talking, but the problem is that I am terrible at expressing myself, which she was well aware of. She had always looked at my eyes and understood what was going on in my head since I was a child. I once asked her how she found out. " A mother knows everything," she explained. "And someone who knows you can easily read your eyes, because your eyes speak louder than you." And I exclaimed, " What a typical Bollywood statement!" We both laughed.

Now coming back to the days when she came from the hospital, she became very weak and was not able to speak, as this was a major surgery. The doctor said that it will take some time for her speech to come back. But I was feeling helpless to see her in this way. Being an emotional person, who loves her family like anything, even in my worst nightmare, I can't see them in pain. I still remember while going to bed, I used to pray to keep my parents healthy, make all their good dreams come true and any pain coming on their way to give it to me and give them all the good things. But now I think that all my prayers were ignored and that too very harshly.

On 7th July Wednesday, the day started with normal activities, everyone in the family was trying to make mum happy and comfortable. That day, her tissue report came, based on this, her next treatment was going to be planned. We were happy that the left tumor had not increased and even the doctor had said that it was a miracle. Our faith in God strengthened.

But....................................

Mom behaved strangely that evening; she lost her senses and had a fever. We immediately tried to contact the doctors, but we ultimately decided to transport her to Tata Memorial Hospital, where she was receiving treatment. My father and sister-in-law accompanied her once again. By that time, Papa had learned that I was in shock, so they both decided that I should stay at home because being around children would allow me to talk, which would help me to be strong.

They arrived at the hospital at midnight and she was admitted right away. I discovered that none of them slept that night because there was nowhere for them to sleep. I felt helpless because both of them were diabetic. The next day, the doctor confirmed that she had a brain infection, which caused her to lose control, become aggressive and go without food. It was a helpless situation for all of us because she would not respond to medicines if she didn't have food.

I received another call from the hospital one day, informing me that my mother had become bedridden and that a food pipe from her nose had been implanted. She was also to be on a liquid diet, according to the doctor. Listening to all of this on a daily basis, I was breaking each and every second. I used to look at her reports online, send them to other doctors, consult with them, and then call my sister-in-law again and again. But I couldn't bring myself to go to the hospital.

One day, when everyone in my family forced me, I went to the hospital. Seeing her, I wanted to burst out in tears, but I said to myself that this is not the time. I hugged my mom, but I think I was not lucky for my mom. That feeling got firm when she was taken to ICU soon after that. Today also I think that if I was not born, she would have been alive and healthy. I was waiting in the waiting lounge, as I was not allowed to go inside. The doctors came to me and said that my mom had a very limited time and anytime, anything could happen, and this had already been said to my father and sister. Listening to all of this, I became very angry, and trust me, I wanted to kill those doctors and thought that they were just doctors, not God . Do they know how much time has been left with them?

Anyway, I made it inside to meet Mom. I took her hands in mine and said, " Mumma, I love you; without you, I am nothing. You are the most important person in my life; in fact, you are my entire life. Please don't leave, you're a fighter; fight and return to prove everyone wrong." She opened her eyes and said, " YES." I was relieved to hear this because she has always kept her promises.

**Days passed, some were fine, some were not, mostly worse, dipping into deep grief.**

There was no place on her body where injection marks did not exist. Her entire body was swollen, but she was determined to recover; this was MY MOTHER. A true fighter never says no and is always self-assured. I remember her telling everyone in ICU, when she was conscious, that her daughter is an engineer, that she is a very good girl, and that she is very proud of her. When she returns home, she will make sure that she marries as soon as possible. She wants to return home as soon as possible because she has identical twin grandsons. As I listened to all of this, I felt helpless and decided to do something.

One day papa called me and said, "Doctors have given their reply. They are saying that if she is going on a ventilator, then it will be very difficult and she may not come back." So what should they do? He was seeking an answer; I had to reply, but I had nothing to say. What do I decide? As there was an infection in the central line, they have to change the direction of the central line too, which is highly dangerous. Listening to all of this over the call, I felt helpless and totally numbed . I took a deep breath and said, " **Let doctors say what they want to say, I have full faith in Siddhi Vinayaka (Lord Ganesh) and he will never do any bad thing." Listening to this, I think papa got a little relieved and told the doctor, " Sir, you are doctors, you know what is good for her. Please make sure that she shows at least some improvements so that we can take her home."**

It was a miracle, yes indeed, it was a miracle, as the doctor said. Mom recovered and was soon shifted to the ward. She was talking and listening to the doctor's command and sleeping at night. Previously she used to stay awake the entire night and yell because she was not in her senses; as per doctors, while operating her they had removed a part of her brain which controlled the senses. But I never believed this to be true, not because I am her daughter, but because of some incidents.

Again, back to the story, on 2nd September, she was discharged from the hospital; this time she came in an ambulance. After so many days, there was a smile on her face and this credit goes to my nephews. In the hospital, she used to take their names. A sign of relief that mom has finally come home and will be around us, which will help her to recover.

I remember going to Tata hospital every Tuesday and Wednesday to show her sugar level reports and to talk to doctors with the hope that maybe some medicine had been found that could save mom's life, as it was one of the largest cancer research institutes.

After coming back from the hospital, I used to stay with her the entire night.

We had distributed our duties; in the morning, my sister-in-law and my father will take care of her, and from 6 in the evening to 6 in the morning, I will. I used to also take care of her in between, whenever I had bandwidth for my office work.

One incident came to mind as I was writing this. Why I used to think she hadn't lost her consciousness, one day I woke up with severe stomach pain. As soon as she found out, she inquired, " What happened?" Consider how a person who has lost their senses is supposed to react if they see someone in pain. Even though she could talk normally, the 15 percent of the tumor that was there in her brain doesn't let her sleep.

By this time, I am sure you all wanted to know what Glioma is. And what are its symptoms?

Be patient. You will come to know soon.

# What is this Glioblastoma?

Glioblastoma, also known as Glioma, is one of the rarest but largest cancerous Brain Tumor. It spreads and grows quickly, frequently causing pressure. The entire medical community is looking for treatments for this, but so far there has been no success. I wish there was some kind of treatment. COPD patients are at high risk, which her doctors were well aware of, but sadly!!!

If I may explain in layman terms, it is a personal summons from God of Death (Yamraj). According to Google, only 5% of patients live longer than five years, but ask their loved ones how they live and what sign of relief their family members take once they are gone, not because they are tired, but because they can see the person whom they love so much in pain.

In Tata hospital, we met a man whose entire head had been amputated from the back, twice, and who was pleading with the doctor for his death; sad but true.

So, before saying the symptoms, I would like to tell you something about my UNIVERSE.

**'It doesn't matter how we are born, but it matters how you leave this world,' because your work, which some call karma, determines how the world knows you.**

My Universe was a self-assured, intelligent, and caring individual. I've never met anyone like her before. Our entire family was together because of her. She taught me that it doesn't matter how successful you are in your career or how many awards you have received; if you can't keep your family together and happy, you are the biggest failure in your life. She was the best mother-in-law, the best sister-in-law, the best mother, the best wife, and the best friend; she was the best in all her relationships.

She had a Master's degree in political science at a time when girls were only allowed to study until the 10th grade. She was even awarded a gold medal. During the pandemic, when the entire world was locked inside the house and some wise people were busy taking selfies, instead of helping others, she secretly helped many poor people, including household workers coming into our complexes, such as household servants, the laundry man who used to iron our clothes, and many more I can't even remember. Not for a few months or a few days, but for over a year, without even family members knowing, not even me. She was the type of person who used to think and care for others, whether she knew that person or not.

Many a time, she used to get hurt and say, "I have done my Karma and another person has done his karma. He is happy for whatever he has done and I am happy for whatever I have done. So in short, we all are happy."

When people began visiting our home and inquiring about her health, we discovered how much she had helped so many. I recall the laundryman telling her that nothing bad would happen to her because poor people's blessings walked along with her. Listening to this, I felt so relieved and proud of her that I can't put it into words.

We were both movie buffs; if a new movie came out, good or bad, we used to watched it and then discussed it in depth. Even our government, I don't think, discussed our country's budget as thoroughly as we did the movies. If they had, the situation today would be different. That is a different topic, which we will address at a later date.

**Well coming back to Symptoms: -**

Watery nose, headache, confusion, forgetting things, mismatch of words, sudden change in attitude, falling unconscious, suffocation, losing balance, stammering; if out of these if any two of these symptoms match, go to the doctor and request a brain scan, an MRI, or a tumor scan. This is the most secure method of detecting a tumor at an early stage.

But why wait for the symptoms to appear? Confused? Allow me to explain: -

On birthdays, we spend thousands of rupees giving parties to our loved ones, but instead of that, why don't we give treat to our body by taking a complete medical test, right from tip to toe, from a blood test to a full-body scan. I am not saying that one should not enjoy their birthdays or should not give a party to their dear ones; I am trying to explain that if anything happens to us, then nobody can share our pain. It is our body which stays with us till our last breath and bears all the pain.

Remember, it's we who are our own best friends, so love yourself and take care of yourself as much as you can.

**Last but not the least, stay away from toxicity, spread happiness and be happy. In the end, what matters the most is how happy you actually are.**

# Trip to Haridwar

**The media has a large influence on everyone, especially on innocent people. They advertise so much that we start believing it.**

Well, this is one of the most interesting incidents, which is also a part of the journey.

My mother used to watch yoga on NDTV India every morning, performed by our very own, very famous YOG GURU, whom he refers to as a True DESH BHAKT. I'm not going to take any names in order to avoid controversy, but I believe you'd figured it out by now. And his influence was so strong that even she wanted to go there for treatment because he used to make grand claims about curing this and that disease. So she wanted to go there with the hope that his treatment would help her lungs recover.

I registered for a 21-day stay after she was discharged from the hospital in February. There is a protocol in place that requires you to submit all of your medical reports if you have any disease, and then you can book the rooms and pay the money if they accept. All of her most recent medical reports had been uploaded. I also stated very clearly in the description that she had COPD.

We were incredibly happy when the doctor gave us the go-ahead, and we hoped that her lungs would be fine. We reserved our train tickets for March 7th. She was overjoyed because she enjoyed traveling, especially by train. Looking at her joy, I was very excited and hopeful that she would be fine because whenever she had a seizure, doctors would take blood from her artery to check the level of $CO_2$ (Carbon dioxide ). Believe me, it was excruciating to witness and experience. I used to think that if seeing is so painful, imagine how much pain the person on whom this test was performed must be in. And this was not a one-time test; it was repeated several times, and only doctors can perform it.

I remember once I heard her saying to somebody that she was alive just because of me and once I settled down, she will die peacefully. I was a college student at the time.

Returning to the trip, we arrived on Monday, March 8th, around 11 a.m. The place where people used to stay was very far away, in a village in Haridwar with no network connectivity. When the doctor saw us, she simply made a diet chart that we had to follow starting the next day.

That day, as we were very tired, we had our dinner which consisted of some bitter gourd juice and something else which I don't remember. The journey began the following day. We awoke at 4 a.m. It started with yoga, then naturopathy, and finally oil massage, where their employees inquired about our whereabouts. They stripped us naked and then began gossiping. It became our responsibility to remind them about the time.Then the steam bath, mud bath, yoga, then lunch, and so on until 9 p.m.

We were ecstatic because during lunch, I noticed that every second person had the same diet chart and therapy chart. No matter which treatment he or she has enrolled, our dearest Babaji sees all diseases with one eye, SHOCKING!

Mom's oxygen level dropped again as a result of the smooth and relaxing treatment of running here and there, and doctors were called. You'll be surprised to learn that there wasn't a single oxygen machine or hospital in that massive complex. The doctors who arrived were unsure of what needed to be done in this case. They brought a steamer with clove oil, which we normally used in our house for coughs and colds. When I asked the doctor that in the advertisement they had promised to treat major diseases, and that was how they treated- giving the same treatment to everyone? And in case you were not able to treat them, then why did you give them the permission to get enrolled in the first place? If that was done by mistake, then yesterday you saw the report, why didn't you tell yesterday? Were you waiting for us to come? I asked many questions but no answer came from the doctor. After many hours, I called the doctor and said, " We don't wish to get treated here, hence we want to go, kindly refund our money." She informed me that money would not be refunded because it is against protocol. I immediately went to the office where all the doctors were sitting and met with the doctor, saying, " Ma'am, the amount is 1 lakh Rupees and the mistake is not on our side; it is on your side." If you are unable to cure a COPD patient, that does not mean you can experiment on her. There's no hospital, no qualified doctor, and no oxygen machine in this massive complex. Who will be held accountable if something happens to my mother? Certainly not us. After nearly two hours of arguing, she agreed to return the money and asked me to visit the head doctor.

After visiting the head doctor's cabin, I saw almost everyone who had been waiting with us in the reception area the day before. They were inside the hospital's administration room, pleading for their money and crying because the hospital's administration was unwilling to return their funds. Some said they believed Babaji and thought he has opened this center not for money, but for the betterment of poor people and society. Some said they had sold their land to come here; others said they had sold their gold in the hope that their loved ones would be fine, but their health deteriorated after only one day of treatment. They begged to be let out of the center. Believe me, the scene was heart-wrenching. I was fortunate to receive my money back.

Everything was still a mess. I only able to go to meet these noble-educated doctors because we had neighbours whose cottage was close to ours. I'm grateful to them because that night would have turned into a nightmare if they hadn't been there. Everyone at home was concerned, especially Dad. Thankfully, I was able to contact my aunt, and after speaking with her, I began crying out of fear because I was alone with my mother and there were no or limited trains to Mumbai for the next few days due to the pandemic.

When my mom's rakhi brother came to know out about the incident, he immediately called my aunt and said he was on his way to pick us up. My aunt and uncle arrived the next day to take us out of that hell, and seeing them was a relief to me.

But the question is, do the media take their roles and responsibilities seriously? Do these noble Babas understand the worth of a person's life?

The reason for this is that we Indians are so emotional that we give someone so much importance that the person inadvertently gains the authority to play with our lives.

There was a time when there was real media and real babas. In this day and age, everyone is after money.

I still remember more than 50% of people came to lose their weight. And, to be honest, why do we need all of these centres to lose weight or get in shape? Why can't we live a healthy, toxin-free lifestyle? Why do we bow our heads in these bogus promises? Why is it so important to lose weight or improve our physical appearance?

The only thing that matters in this universe is that you are happy. This is something I've learned after losing a lot of things in my life. Finally, I would say, 'Stay away from anyone who judges you based on your physical appearance, because that person is a CERTIFIED TOXIC PERSON,' and such people are like ACID; once you let them into your life, they will completely destroy you. Also, avoid all of these NOBLE BABAs because they are only here to make money, not to heal you.

I apologise if I offend anyone, but the truth is bitter.

# Hope

**The biggest cage and the biggest weapon for any fight is HOPE.**

**This word gives you hope that everything will be fine one day, but it also prevents you from seeing the reality.**

I still remember when doctors used to come into our room and used to inform us about mom's health. We used to see them with blank faces and teary eyes. Mostly mom used to stay in the ICU and we used to wait in the reception area, seeing other people crying and praying, calling their family members, trying to get emotional support. In Tata Memorial hospital, it is written everywhere to believe in HOPE, but nobody says till when?

If you want to see how this devil (Cancer) destroys everything and breaks a family so badly, that in everything they see, they think about this devil. If anybody sneezes in their family, they get afraid. Ask a family who has gone through all this. Why 'Cancer' can't just stay only in our zodiac sign? Another incident occurred while Mom was in ICU and I was waiting in the reception area when a woman sitting next to me inquired about my mother. I learned from her that she had lost her husband to this disease two years ago. She was expecting a child at the time; now, two years later, her child has the same disease and is in the intensive care unit. She was sobbing uncontrollably; she continued telling her story about how the doctors had given her the answer, but she is still hopeful that nothing bad will happen to her child because God is not so cruel.

Many days passed, half of my family were in hospital and half in home, but the pain and fear were the same; losing Mumma. Each one of us was begging God and doctors. Each one of us was having only one dream; one day a miracle will happen and Mumma will be fine. God is not so cruel that he will destroy one family, a family that is begging, crying each second. An old man who has not left his wife alone for a second, a daughter-in-law who loves her mother-in-law more than her mother, a daughter who has lost her sense completely, grandsons who have suddenly become mature at the age of 8, and a son who is secretly crying and praying. Seeing our love for Mumma, even the doctors used to pray so our family does not break, because even they could see and feel that if something happens to her, our family will be shattered.

I used to tell Mom that nothing bad would happen to her. We have overcome many obstacles in our lives, and we will overcome this one as well; we just need to be confident and not to give up.

Whenever she was fully conscious, she would ask me if I had someone in mind for marriage. If so, please hurry. Listening to her, I used to curse myself, wondering what kind of daughter I am that I am unable to fulfil my mother's wish. I had fulfilled all of her wishes, so why can't I do this? But I used to tell myself, 'Be hopeful, and everything will be fine.'

I felt alone on this journey because it was the first time I had been extremely afraid and Mumma was not present. But I used to comfort myself by repeatedly telling myself that nothing bad would happen to my mother. This thought used to give me tremendous strength to fight, but deep down I was scared of losing her. We humans use this word 'Hope' because it feels like a saviour during difficult times, when someone abandons or hurts us.

I, sometimes, think that this word is created by doctors, so that patient and their relatives stay calm and allow them to peacefully do their job. More often than not, you find a Mr Angel whose name is Hope. Just imagine, if Mr HOPE was a human being, then he would have been on the wanted list of every person and must have charged anybody who wanted to use his name. After watching the Indian serial where a man has jumped from the 50th floor and another person is saying that he is hopeful that nothing will happen to him, poor Mr Hope must have sued many TV serial markers for misusing his name.

# Contract Marriage

**Sometimes we have to walk down a path that we didn't intend to walk down. .**

After seeing my mother's health and learning her final wish, as well as listening to everyone who claimed to be my mother's well-wisher; best friend, best of buddies, I decided to take bold step. I thought that by doing so, she would be happy, which would aid her recovery. Because life had given her such short notice.

I recall searching for a groom on a matrimony website, and the matches that came up were not like the type of person my mother wanted for me, because if I married any Ena, Meena, or Deeka, all of her hard work to raise me would've been in vain. Also, it would not have helped to  recover.

One fine day, I decided that she had given me this life, and it was now my turn to repay her. So I decided to enter into a contract marriage with the type of person my mother desired for me. Believe me, finding a good person for a serious marriage is difficult, but for a contract marriage, you will receive many good proposals, thanks to our Bollywood, which openly promotes this type of culture.In this type of marriage, You are not entitled to alimony after the contract has over. I knew it was against my ethics because I come from a family where relationships are valued and not exploited for financial gain, but I had no choice.

I'm not sure how Papa found out that I want to marry as soon as possible. I'm not sure what made him say, " Beta, your mom wanted you to fly and reach the sky because she loves you a lot; any wrong step will break her and also me. Reconsider what you're thinking and don't listen to anyone; you're a strong girl and a pillar of our family."'

Normally, my father and I don't talk much, but that day, I realized how much my dad thinks about me and how much he loves me.

In our society, fathers have a macho image in which they never express their emotions or show their children how much they love them. I wish all dads reading this would start expressing their love and care for their children, especially towards their daughters, because when they are having a bad day, they look at you and your one smile keeps reminding them that you are always there for her. It's a request; don't put up a BARRIER.

After listening to my father, the thought of this nonsense marriage vanished as if it had never existed. But these people's words continue to ring in my ears every second. 'If you were so concerned about her, why didn't you fulfil her dream while she was still alive?' But, at the time, when these things were said, Mom was still alive. It's not that I care about society or the people who said it; it's that they dared to say it using my mother's health as an excuse, which I'm sure no child would like.

To all the daughters reading this, even if such a thought arises in you, talk to your father or any other father- figure in your life. Never let society rule your life because it is your life and it belongs only to your family and loved ones.

# The Last Day of Faith

**Life is unpredictable; it abandons you just when you need it the most.**

I remember fasting on Tuesdays because someone once told me that if you fast on Tuesdays and pray to Lord Ganapati, your wishes will come true. I used to fast and pray with a lot of faith, saying, 'I am looking up to you with a lot of faith, please do some MIRACLE, you have to bless her, she needs your blessing. She is the strand that connects us all; please perform miracles.' I used to pray every day, not just on Tuesdays. But I think God was on vacation when I was praying. On the night of the $27^{th}$, Mom vomited while she was wearing a BiPAP. Before you think about what it is, let me tell you, it is a medical device that supports the lungs for breathing. Normally COPD patients use this. That night, I still wonder, how I fell asleep and Mom vomited into her mask. I still curse myself for this and will never forgive myself. Sorry, Mumma, I still wonder how I fell asleep, and believe me I still punish myself for this, if possible please forgive me. The next day, early in the morning, as per the doctor's suggestion, some blood tests were done and I went to Tata Hospital to request the chest specialist to consult Mumma over the phone as the previous day, I had paid for the online consultation. But as soon as the doctor saw her over the call, he immediately asked me to get her admitted to any nearby hospital. For medicines, he said he will call the hospital doctors.

I recall calling dozens of doctors to come to my house that day. I was willing to pay whatever they demanded. However, today's doctors are so insensitive that they don't understand the gravity of the situation and simply say no. One doctor told me that he doesn't want to come because it would take 30 minutes and he would have to take some sort of transportation. That day, I literally begged some doctors to give me a reference of other doctors who can pay a home visit. Some doctors hung up the phone, while others said they couldn't come because of covid.

Finally, we decided that we will call an ambulance and will take her to the Central Railway Hospital, as dad is a government employee and he is entitled to free medical facilities; another reason was no hospital was ready to take her case. Luckily, we were able to get the ambulance and I, along with my dad, went to the hospital. Before going to the hospital, I held her hand and said " I know you are bearing this pain for me, please don't do this. I promise you that I will take care of myself and will fulfil all your dreams ." But now I think, why did I said this? Why did I make this promise? That day, from the morning I didn't has a sip of water, as it was Tuesday and I was fasting for her. It was my 15th Tuesday. As soon as we reached the hospital, the doctor said that she was critical and soon she was shifted to the pre- Covid ward as per their 'PROTOCOL'. My fight with the hospital staff and the management started as , on one side they said that she was critical but on the other side, they shifted my mom to the pre- Covid ward, even though her Covid Antigen test result was NEGATIVE.

Soon, because of these escalations with the staff, she was shifted to the ICU and her ECG was performed which didn't come out well. They sent an orthopedics doctor. I quarreled, 'If the ECG wasn't good, why aren't you sending a cardiologist?' After making a ruckus, a physician came and started pressing her heart. Soon, dad told me that **MOM IS NO MORE.**

Listening to this, I screamed my lungs out saying, 'MUMMA!' and pressed her heart, kissed her forehead, rubbed her hands and feet, kept my head over her heart, hugged her tightly, and did not allow anyone to touch her. I screamed as loudly as I could so that my voice could reach to the God of Death and he could have mercy on me and return my Mom. I was still waiting for the MIRACLE which didn't happen. I was forcefully taken away from my mom, so that hospital staff could tie my Mom. From outside the glass door, I was seeing everything. At one point, I felt that she was breathing but nobody believed me. $28^{th}$ September, 3:55 PM was the black day of my life which snatched everything from me.

That day, for the first time and the last time, I hugged my papa when I saw him crying. It is not that I don't want to hug him next time, but next time, I don't want to hug him in sorrow. I still think that if my mom was treated properly that day, she would have lived longer.

If humans are a big SAMPLE, if any human breaks our trust, we stop talking to him and start hating that person . But if God does that same thing, we say that he must be having a plan. Not because we believe in him, but because we don't have any other alternative. That day, my trust was broken , I was broken from inside very badly as now I was alone in this world. Suddenly there was a feeling that everything had finished, there was darkness everywhere but, at that same moment, I looked at dad with wet eyes, yet standing there as a pillar. Suddenly, a sense of responsibility arose in me and I realized that I had lost Mom but I can't lose my Dad at any cost. I know it will be very difficult to communicate and manage, but I will have to do this. I can't leave him alone.

I knew that life without Mom will be difficult, but I had no idea that it will be so difficult.

**The best way to know what another person thinks about you is to talk in your low phase.**

Within a few hours, Mom's cremation was done and I was in her room when a woman entered. She was one of our long-distance relatives who lived nearby. I cried and said, ' I will make all of my Mom's dreams come true." She, very heartlessly replied, " If you were so concerned about her, then why didn't you get married when she was alive?" It felt that she hated me all these years and was waiting for such an opportunity. Marriage was one of her dreams for me and to make that come true, nobody knows what I had done. That day, I slept near her bedside.

This blaming game never stopped; it was continued in the prayer meeting too.

Our society has become so insensitive that we don't even realize what we are saying and where we are saying it. We have kept so much bitterness for others, that too for no reason, that whenever we get the chance to make that person feel down, we quickly grab it without thinking that by doing this, we are spoiling our Karma and making another person's Karma good.

This incident continued for many days, that too in front of my family. I wondered why my family didn't react. Then, one day my elder brother said that we know who you are and what you are. The people who are telling you these things are spineless and as we cannot insult them, we should ignore them. Try to ignore them as we know you. If you cry, mom will be hurt.

**If you can't share someone's pain, I request you, don't increase that, it is a SIN.**

# We Indians

**'Live and let live,' as the old adage goes.**

But we Indians do the exact opposite. In India, almost every home has a scientist, and many of them have no formal education. We are so jugadu that we can make the most unique things out of anything, leaving NASA researchers scratching their heads. Nonetheless, our country is regressing. Why? Who is to blame for this? I agree that there are many factors, but one of the most important is our mentality.

You must be upset, but it's true. Someone correctly stated, 'Energy is energy; it is up to you whether you want to invest positively or negatively.' Unfortunately, many of us invest negatively by gossiping, busy in making others feel down, commenting on genders, discussing caste, age, and some NOBLE people are busy in making others' lives HELL. So, if we are so busy doing all of these good things, when will we have time to grow in life?

Let's take the example of Priyanka and Nick Jonas's marriage. Where the bride was 10 years OLDER than the groom. When the entire world was busy giving blessings to the couple, we were busy making memes, that too, in a very creative way. Just imagine, if such KIND of people used their talent in the right way then how good their lives would have been. As time is passing, we need to build a wall, a wall of determination and dedication, and promise ourselves that we are not making our life toxic but others' lives too.

If a groom is more than a decade older than a bride, everyone happily attends and praises their marriage, but don't you think we sound hypocritical?

Our dear uncles and aunties are so preoccupied with gossiping about other children that they have no idea what their own child is up to. The funniest part is that in our country, regardless of how dark their child is, every parent wants a fair bride or groom for their child. But, as I've said before, our country is full of shady characters, but this obsession with fairness is so strong that these swindlers make millions by making false promises. If their products are so effective, why don't they sell them in other countries such as Africa? Because they are well aware that those people are very intelligent and are well aware of their situation, and their company will suffer significant losses.

Many rules and laws have been established, but thousands of ways to violate them have been devised. We are so preoccupied with making others feel bad that we have lost sight of what we have accomplished with our lives.

We have set age criteria for everything, such as girls getting married until the age of 25 because they will not be able to have children after that. But who has been entrusted with the responsibility of defining this thing? Many couples marry at a young age and do not have children, and many couples marry after the age of 30 and have children. Who has asked you to be God and make decisions for others? Let them live because it is their choice and their life.

We say we respect girls in India, but do we really? In our country, many people assassinate a girl's character in front of everyone, and what do we do to defend her? We simply stand in a corner and watch the show. But is that correct?

Currently, one word, 'KARMA,' is trending in the market. But have we done any significant karma to determine the eligibility criteria for anyone? The answer is NO.

I am proud to be an Indian, but I cannot encourage the bullying that we engage in, both consciously and unconsciously. Our country is known as a land of relationships, where family and friendship are valued, but you might be surprised to learn that one in every twenty people suffers from depression as a result of this harassing attitude toward them. Is this correct?

Almost everyone is concerned about SOCIETY, and we are so concerned about these intangible people that many things in life that we would like to do go unfulfilled. Many love stories go untold, and many dreams die without even being tried. But why is that? Why can't we do the things we really want to do? We act responsibly, so why can't we hear the cries for help from those around us? Why do we simply ignore and move on? The reason is that we don't care about anyone; in our rush to make money and impress others, we've forgotten that we are HUMANS and showing humanity to others is our first responsibility.

If you see someone who is different from others, who has strange dreams, or who is trying to make their loved one's dreams come true, please don't JUDGE them because if you can't support someone, please don't let them down. Because it only takes 5 minutes for you to say or write something stupid on any social media platform, but the impact lasts a lifetime. It makes no difference how powerful that person is. But you know deep down that this isn't true. So, why are you wasting your time doing this?

**A Roaster: -**

Our uncles and aunts are gossip kings and queens. One day, this group of noble people was sitting in a park, without a mask, gossiping when Corona happened to pass by. When he saw them without a mask, he decided to say hello, passed beside them, and then fainted after listening to their conversation. Our poor Corona was admitted to the ICU after being infected with GOSVID, a virus that combines gossip and hate . When he awoke, he saw those people and began screaming and yelling for help. When the doctors arrived and saw that he was seeking help, they were surprised and asked, 'you are the most dangerous virus that has engulfed the entire world in fear, so who can make you afraid?' 'I take lives, but this GOSVID takes a person's self-confidence and refuses to let them die,' he said. So, morally, these people are DANGEROUS, even more so than I am.'

**END**

www.ingramcontent.com/pod-product-compliance
Ingram Content Group UK Ltd.
Pitfield, Milton Keynes, MK11 3LW, UK
UKHW021644190726
13853UKWH00001B/43

9 789393 809896